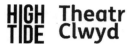 

C000184978

HighTide and Theatr Clwyd present

HEROINE

A world premiere by Nessah Muthy

Supported by
The Carne Trust

Heroine premiered at HighTide Festival Aldeburgh on 13 September 2017.
Heroine then transferred to the Sherman Theatre from 19–23 September, then HighTide
Festival Walthamstow from 27 September–8 October before transferring to Theatr
Clwyd from 18 October–4 November in a production directed by Steven Atkinson,
Artistic Director of HighTide.

Supported using public funding by
**ARTS COUNCIL
ENGLAND**

HEROINE

HighTide and Theatr Clwyd present

GRACE	Asmara Gabrielle
BEVERLEY	Maggie McCarthy
CHERYL	Wendy Morgan
WENDY	Lucy Thackeray
SHELLEY	Hannah Traylen

Director	Steven Atkinson
Design	Richard Kent
Lighting	Elliot Griggs
Sound Designer	Adrienne Quartly
Dramaturgical Support	Abigail Gonda, Carissa Hope Lynch
Casting Director	Louis Hammond CDG
Assistant Director	Charlotte Fraser
Production Manager	Heather Doole
Stage Manager	Roisin Symes
Costume Supervisor	Ryan Walklett

CAST

ASMARA GABRIELLE | GRACE
Theatre includes: *Pimp Bobby* (Leicester Square).

Film includes: *Finding Fatimah* (BMTV); *My Abuse* (Focus Media); *How to Succeed* (Bodiam Pictures).

MAGGIE McCARTHY | BEVERLEY
Theatre includes: *Silver Lining* (English Touring Theatre/Rose, Kingston); *We Wait in Joyful Hope* (Theatre503); *Juno and the Paycock* (Bristol Old Vic/Liverpool Theatres); *Private Lives* (Chichester Festival Theatre); *Absence of War* (Headlong/Rose, Kingston/Sheffield Theatres); *Children of the Sun, Cocktail Sticks, Mother Clap's Molly House* (National Theatre).

Television includes: *Dancing on the Edge* (BBC); *Call the Midwife* (BBC/Neal Street Productions); *Coronation Street* (Granada Television).

Film credits include *Angela's Ashes* (Scott Rudin Productions); *Attack the Block* (ATB Productions); *The History Boys* (BBC Two Films); *Calendar Girls* (Harbour Pics); *Ghost Stories* (Wrap Films).

WENDY MORGAN | CHERYL
Theatre includes: *Animal Farm, Martine* (Olivier and Standard Best Actress nominations); *Yonadab, As I Lay Dying, Bacchai, A Streetcar Named Desire, Phedre* (National Theatre); *Hatched and Dispatched* (Park).

Film includes: *Yanks* (Most Promising Newcomer Award); *Birth of The Beatles; 84 Charing X Road; The Mirror Crack'd*.

Television includes: *The Jewel in the Crown* (Granada TV); *Midsomer Murders* (Bentley Productions); *Casualty* (BBC); *Wire in the Blood, Emmerdale* (ITV).

LUCY THACKERAY | WENDY
Lucy Thackeray recently appeared in *Alginate* at the Bunker Theatre.

Other theatre includes: *A Midsummer Night's Dream* (Shakespeare's Globe); *My Beautiful Black Dog* (Bush); *Bike* (Salisbury Playhouse).

Television includes: *Damned* (Channel 4); *New Tricks, Casualty* (BBC); *The Five* (Red Productions for Sky).

HANNAH TRAYLEN | SHELLEY
Hannah Traylen graduated from Italia Conti last year and is making her professional stage debut.

Theatre credits whilst at drama school include: *Coram Boy, The Libertine, Time and the Conways, Three Sisters, Twelfth Night* (Italia Conti); *Oliver Twist* (Italia Conti/Edinburgh Fringe) and *God Bless Ye Merry Gentleman* (Grindstone, Tristan Bates).

Television includes: *Howards End* (BBC/Starz); *Doctors* (BBC); *Harlots* (ITV Encore); *Call the Midwife* (BBC/Neal Street Productions); *Unforgotten* (ITV).

CREATIVES

NESSAH MUTHY | WRITER

Nessah Muthy is a writer for TV and theatre. She has written for Cardboard Citizens, National Youth Theatre and the Royal Court Theatre. Nessah is under commission to the Kali Theatre and the National Youth Theatre. For screen, Nessah has written for *Holby City*, following successful completion of the show's shadow scheme, and has previously written for *EastEnders: E20* and currently developing an original television drama for the BBC Drama Writers' Programme.

STEVEN ATKINSON | DIRECTOR

Steven Atkinson is co-founder and the Artistic Director of HighTide Theatre.

Directing for HighTide includes: *In Fidelity* (Traverse); *The Sugar-Coated Bullets of the Bourgeoisie* (Arcola); *Forget Me Not* (Bush); *So Here We Are* (Royal Exchange); *Lampedusa* (Soho); *peddling* (Arcola/Off-Broadway); *Pussy Riot: Hunger Strike* (Bush/Southbank Centre); *Neighbors* (Nuffield); *Bottleneck* (Soho/ UK tour); *Clockwork; Bethany; Incoming; Dusk Rings A Bell* (Watford Palace); *Lidless* (Trafalgar Studios); *Muhmah* (HighTide Festival) and *The Pitch* (Latitude).

Other theatre includes: *Chicken* (Paines Plough Roundabout); *The Afghan and the Penguin* (Radio 4).

HEATHER DOOLE | PRODUCTION MANAGER

Heather is a freelance production manager.

Her previous credits include: *Origins Festival* (Border Crossings); *Becoming* (Donmar Warehouse Rehearsal Studio); *Assata Taught Me, The Convert, I Call My Brothers, Diary of a Madman* and *The Iphigenia Quartet* (Gate).

Deputy production manager credits include: *Up Next!* (National Theatre); *Platinum, Giving, The Argument, The Meeting, 36 Phone Calls, Sunspots, Deluge, Deposit, Elephants, State Red* (Hampstead Downstairs); *Carmen* (Blackheath Halls); *No Villain* (Trafalgar Studios/Old Red Lion); *Radiant Vermin* (59E59, New York/Soho, London/Tobacco Factory, Bristol); *All or Nothing* (The Vaults); *Firebird, Kiss Me* (Hampstead Downstairs/Trafalgar Studios); *4000 Days, Grounded* (Park); *Four Minutes Twelve Seconds* (Trafalgar Studios); *The Session* (Soho); *Octagon* (Arcola); *And Then Came The Nightjars* (Bristol Old Vic Studio/Theatre503); *Valhalla, Animals, Cinderella and the Beanstalk* (Theatre503) and *Women Centre Stage Festival* (NT Temporary Space/Hampstead).

Heather assisted on *Bull* (Young Vic).

CHARLOTTE FRASER | ASSISTANT DIRECTOR

Charlotte is studying for an MFA in Theatre Directing at Birkbeck University, and will be on placement with HighTide in 2017/18.

Prior to this she studied English at university, where she produced and directed for the student new-writing festival and assistant directed at the Oxford Playhouse. She was a reader for the Finborough Theatre (2014–16) and is a member of Healing Minds, a collective who use theatre workshops to facilitate conversation around mental health.

ELLIOT GRIGGS | LIGHTING

Elliot Griggs trained at RADA.

For HighTide: *The Sugar-Coated Bullets of the Bourgeoisie, Lampedusa.*

Theatre includes: *Loot* (Park/Watermill); *Kiki's Delivery Service* (Southwark Playhouse); *Disco Pigs* (Trafalgar Studios); *Hir, Forget Me Not* (Bush); *The Oracles* (Punchdrunk); *An Octoroon, Low Level Panic, Sheppey, buckets* (Orange Tree); *Home Truths, Benefit* (Cardboard Citizens); *Diminished, The Argument, Deluge* (Hampstead); *Don't Wake the Damp, He Had Hairy Hands, The Boy Who Kicked Pigs* (Soho/Lowry/UK tour); *Faust X2* (Watermill); *Raising Martha* (Park); *Fleabag* (Soho/UK tour); *Fool for Love* (Found 111); *Romeo and Juliet, Pigeon English* (NYT); *My Eyes Went Dark* (Traverse/Finborough); *Educating Rita* (Hull Truck); *The Night Watch* (Royal Exchange); *Martha, Josie and the Chinese Elvis* (Bolton Octagon/Hull Truck); *Yen* (Royal Court/Royal Exchange); *Pomona* (National Theatre/Royal Exchange/Orange Tree; Off West End Award for Best Lighting Designer); *John Ferguson, The Soft of Her Palm, And I and Silence* (Finborough).

Event design includes *Height of Winter, The Single-Opticon, Alcoholic Architecture* (Bompas & Parr).

LOUIS HAMMOND CDG | CASTING DIRECTOR

For HighTide: *Heroine* (HighTide Festival/Theatr Clwyd); *The Sugar-Coated Bullets of the Bourgeoisie* (Arcola/HighTide Festival); *Harrogate* (HighTide Festival/Royal Court/House).

Theatre includes: *The 5 Plays Project, Creditors, The Member of the Wedding, Dirty Butterfly, The Indian Wants the Bronx* (Young Vic); *Inkheart, The Funfair, Romeo and Juliet* (HOME Manchester); *The Distance* (Sheffield Crucible/Orange Tree); *Romeo and Juliet* (Sheffield Crucible); *Primetime, Violence and Son, Who Cares, Fireworks* (Casting Associate at the Royal Court); *Amadeus* (Chichester Festival Theatre); *The Winter's Tale* (Regent's Park Open Air); *The History Boys* (Sheffield Crucible); *Driving Miss Daisy* (UK tour); *Batman Live* (world arena tour); *The Trial of Dennis the Menace* (Southbank Centre); *The Resistible Rise of Arturo Ui* (Liverpool Playhouse/Nottingham Playhouse); *Blue/Orange* (Arcola); *Von Ribbentrop's Watch* (UK tour); *Mrs Reynolds and the Ruffian, Brighton Beach Memoirs, Absent Friends* (Watford Palace); *All My Sons* (Curve, Leicester); 50th Anniversary Season of 50 Rehearsed Readings, Caryl Churchill Season, International Residencies and new writers' Rough Cuts presentations (Royal Court); *Loot* (Tricycle); *Blowing Whistles* (Leicester Square); *Testing the Echo* (Tricycle Theatre/Out of Joint tour); *The Importance of Being Earnest* (UK tour/ Vaudeville); *Donkeys' Years* (UK tour); *Rock'n'Roll* (Royal Court/Duke of York's); *Jus' Like That* (Garrick).

Louis was Head of Casting at *The Bill* (Thames TV), and also cast films *Arsene Lupin, Ne Quittez Pas, Beyond Re-Animator* and *Mirrormask.*

He is a member of the Casting Directors' Guild of Great Britain and Ireland.

RICHARD KENT | DESIGNER

For HighTide: *Clockwork* (HighTide Festival); *Neighbors* (HighTide Festival/Nuffield).

Theatre includes: *The Country Girls* (Chichester Festival Theatre); *Dead Funny* (Vaudeville); *Murder Ballad* (Arts); *Unfaithful* (Found111); *Oliver* (Grange Park Opera); *Watership Down* (Watermill); *The Winter's Tale*, *Cymbeline* (Shakespeare's Globe); *The Cocktail Party* (Print Room at the Coronet); *The Mentalists* (Wyndham's); *Communicating Doors* (Menier Chocolate Factory); *Outside Mullingar* (Theatre Royal Bath); *Man to Man* (Wales Millenium Centre); *Multitudes*, *The Colby Sisters of Pittsburgh, Pennsylvania*, *A Boy and His Soul*, *Paper Dolls* (Tricycle); *Anything Goes*, *This Is My Family* (Sheffield Crucible/UK tour); *Bad Jews* (Ustinov Bath/St James/ Arts/Haymarket/UK tour); *Handbagged* (Tricycle/Vaudeville/UK tour); *The Merchant of Venice* (Singapore Repertory Theatre); *The El.Train* (Hoxton Hall); *Mrs Lowry and Son* (Trafalgar Studios 2); *Macbeth*, *Sheffield Mysteries* (Sheffield Crucible); *The Dance of Death* (Donmar Trafalgar); *Josephine Hart Poetry Week* (ARTS); *13* (NYMT, Apollo); *Titanic – Scenes from the British Wreck Commissioners Inquiry: 1912* (MAC Theatre, Belfast); *Richard II* (Donmar Warehouse); *Mixed Marriage* (Finborough); *Decline and Fall* (Old Red Lion); *Stronger and Pariah* (Arcola); *Gin and Tonic and Passing Trains* (Tramway, Glasgow).

Richard worked as Associate to Christopher Oram from 2008–2012.

ADRIENNE QUARTLY | SOUND

Sound design includes: *Rose* (Home Manchester); *The Crucible*, *Partners In Crime* (Queen's, Hornchurch); *The Here And This And Now*, *Merit*, *The Whipping Man* (Theatre Royal Plymouth); *Cuttin' It* (Young Vic/Royal Court); *Opening Skinner's Box* (Improbable); *I Am Thomas* (National Theatre of Scotland); *Bad Jews* (Theatre Royal Haymarket); *Splendour* (Donmar Warehouse); *A Raisin in the Sun*, *One Monkey Don't Stop No Show* (Eclipse); *The Ghost Train*, *Too Clever By Half*, *You Can't Take It With You* (Royal Exchange, Manchester); *Get Happy* (Barbican); *The Ladykillers* (Watermill); *After Electra* (Tricycle); *Sex and the Three Day Week* (Liverpool Everyman); *Grand Guignol* (Southwark Playhouse/Drum, Plymouth); *Untold Stories* (West Yorkshire Playhouse); *Every Last Trick* (Spymonkey); *Tale of Two Cities*, *My Zinc Bed*, *Private Fears in Public Places*, *Just Between Ourselves*, *Habeas Corpus*, *Quartermaine's Terms* (Royal & Derngate); *Inside Wagner's Head* (Linbury, Royal Opera House); *Fräuline Julie (After August)* (Barbican/Schaubühne); *Rings of Saturn* (Halle Kalk, Cologne); *Body of an American*, *Tejas Verdes* (Gate); *Here Lies Mary Spindler* (RSC); *The Container*, *The Shawl* (Young Vic); *Stockholm* (Frantic Assembly); *365* (National Theatre of Scotland); *The Roundabout* season (Paines Plough); *And The Horse You Rode* (Barbican Bite Festival); *93.2fm* (Royal Court); *4000 Miles* (Ustinov, Bath); *The Fastest Clock In The Universe* (Hampstead); *Woyzeck* (St. Ann's Warehouse, New York); *The Importance of Being Earnest* (Rose, Kingston/ Hong Kong Festival); *The Vortex* (Rose, Kingston); *Chekhov In Hell*, *The Astronaut's Chair*, *Nostalgia* (Drum, Plymouth).

Sound and composition credits include: *I'd Rather Goya Robbed Me of My Sleep Than Some Other Arsehole* (Gate); *The Tragedy of Thomas Hobbes* (RSC).

Composition credits include: *The Whipping Man* (Drum, Plymouth); *Faustus*, *The School for Scandal*, *Volpone*, *The Duchess of Malfi* (Stage On Screen/Greenwich); *Rumpelstiltskin* (Norwich Puppet Theatre); *Three Little Pigs*, *The Balloon Gardener*, *Lighter Than Air* (Circo Ridiculoso); *Dream Story* (Gate); *A Christmas Carol* (Sherman Cymru); *The Painter*, *Enemy of the People* (Arcola).

ROISIN SYMES | STAGE MANAGER

Theatre credits include: *Hir* (Bush); *Big Guns* (The Yard); *Kiki's Delivery Service, Orca, Eye of a Needle, Superior Donuts* (Southwark Playhouse); *House/Amongst The Reeds* (Clean Break/The Yard); *After Independence* (Arcola); *The Bear* (Polka/Albany Deptford); *Love Birds – The Musical* (Pleasance Edinburgh); *Unearthed* (UK tour); *Donkey Heart* (Trafalgar Studios/Old Red Lion); *Coolatully, Unscorched* (Finborough); *The Matchgirls* (Wilton's Music Hall); *The Magpies, The Wolves* (Tristan Bates); *Many Moons* (Theatre503).

A MAJOR PLATFORM
FOR NEW PLAYWRIGHTS

HighTide is a theatre company.

We produce new plays in an annual festival in Aldeburgh (Suffolk) & Walthamstow (London) and on tour.

Our programming influences the mainstream. Our work takes place in the here and now.

HighTide: Adventurous theatre for adventurous people

Supported using public funding by
**ARTS COUNCIL
ENGLAND**

LANSONS
Advice Ideas Results

BackstageTrust

H|GH T|DE

2017

OVER A DECADE OF INFLUENCING THE MAINSTREAM

Our eleventh HighTide Festival premiered new works by Sam Steiner and Nessah Muthy as well as returning work from Theresa Ikoko.

All three productions featured at HighTide Festival, Aldeburgh before transferring to HighTide Festival, Walthamstow for the first time.

Nessah Muthy's debut production **Heroine,** transferred to Theatr Clwyd and Sherman Theatre following its premiere at HighTide Festival 2017.

Sam Steiner's **Kanye The First** transferred to North Wall Arts Centre and The Marlowe Theatre following its premiere at HighTide Festival 2017.

We were delighted to welcome back **Girls** by Theresa Ikoko after its successful debut in 2016. **Girls** opened as part of the British Council Showcase at the Edinburgh Fringe Festival 2017 before returning to HighTide Festival. Following HighTide Festival, the production transferred to Salisbury Playhouse and The Drum, Theatre Royal Plymouth.

For full details, visit hightide.org.uk

H|GH
T|DE

24a St John Street, London, EC1M 4AY
0207 566 9765 - hello@hightide.org.uk - hightide.org.uk

HighTide Company
Artistic Director Steven Atkinson
Festival Producer Paul Jellis
Associate Director Andrew Twyman
Birkbeck Assistant Director Charlotte Fraser

Executive Producer Francesca Clar~
General Manager Robyn Keynes
Administrator Holly White
Channel 4 Playwright Theresa Ikok~

First Commissions: Writers on Attachment
16/17: Jon Barton; Sophie Ellerby; Healah Riazi; Nina Segal; Christopher York.
17/18: Harry Davies; Tim Foley; Olivia Hirst; Ellie Kendrick; Isley Lynn; Milly Thomas

Associate Artists
Rosy Banham; Tinuke Craig; Ng Choon Ping; Eleanor Rhode; Roy Alexander Weise

In 2017 - 18 HighTide has collaborated with
Paul Jellis; Martha Rose Wilson; Soho Theatre; Talawa Theatre Company,; Theatr Clwyd; Chichester Festival Theatre; New Wolsey Theatre; North Wall Arts Centre; The Marlowe Theatre; Sherman Theatre; Salisbury Playhouse; The Drum; Theatre Royal Plymouth

Board
Steven Atkinson; Tim Clark (Chair); Nancy Durrant; Sue Emmas; Liz Fosbury; Jon Gilchrist; Diana Hiddleston; Priscilla John; Clare Parsons; Vinay Patel; John Rodgers; Leah Schmidt; Graham White (Deputy Chair)

Festival Board
Robin Boyd; Tallulah Brown; Andrew Clarke; Joyce Hytner OBE; Heather Newill; Ruth Proctor; Dallas Smith; Jenni Wake-Walker; Roger Wingate; Caroline Wiseman

Patrons
Sinead Cusack; Stephen Daldry CBE; Sir Richard Eyre CBE; Sally Greene OBE; Sir David Hare; Sir Nicholas Hytner; Sam Mendes CBE; Juliet Stevenson CBE.

H|GH T|DE

WE NEED YOUR SUPPORT

There are very talented young playwrights in the UK, and if they are lucky they will find their way to the HighTide FestivalTheatre season in Suffolk. I hope you will join me in supporting this remarkable and modest organisation. With your help HighTide can play an even more major role in the promoting of new writing in the UK.

— Lady Susie Sainsbury, Backstage Trust

HighTide is a registered charity and we could not champion the next generation of theatre artists and create world-class productions for you without ticket sales, fundraising, sponsorship and public investment.

To undertake our work this year we need to raise over £750,000.

We need your help to make these targets. You can show your support by: making a donation; buying Festival tickets; recommending the Festival to your friends; donating your time to help work on the Festival; writing to your local councillor and MPs about how much you value the HighTide Festival.

If you would like to discuss making a donation to HighTide, please speak to francesca@hightide.org.uk or call on 0207 566 9765.

We are thankful to all of our supporters, without whom our work simply would not take place.

HighTide Theatre is a National Portfolio Organisation of the Arts Council England

Leading Partner: Lansons

Major Funder: Backstage Trust

Trusts and Foundations
Adnams Charitable Foundation; The Channel 4 Playwrights Scheme, The Carne Trust, The Eranda Rothschild Foundation, Garrick Charitable Trust, Harold Hyam Wingate Foundation, The John Thaw Foundation, The Martin Bowley Charitable Trust, The Noël Coward Foundation, Parham Trust, Peter Wolff Theatre Trust; Suffolk Community Foundation

Individual Supporters
Tim and Caroline Clark, Sam Fogg, Jan Hall, Diana Hiddleston, Tony Mackintosh and Criona Palmer, Clare Parsons and Tony Langham, Leah Schmidt, Mark and Deirdre Simpson, Lord and Lady Stevenson, Graham and Sue White.

Corporate Sponsors
Neil Ewen and all at Central Estates ActIV, The Agency, Central Estates Fullers, Lancasters' Home & Garden, United Agents.

Theatr
Clwyd

'One of the hidden treasures of North Wales, a huge vibrant culture complex'

Guardian

Theatr Clwyd is one of the foremost producing theatres in Wales – a beacon of excellence looking across the Clwydian Hills yet only forty minutes from Liverpool.

Since 1976 we have been a theatrical powerhouse and much-loved home for our community. Now, led by the new Executive team of Tamara Harvey and Liam Evans-Ford, we are going from strength to strength producing world-class theatre, from new plays to classic revivals.

We have three theatres, a cinema, café, bar and art galleries and, alongside our own shows, offer a rich and varied programme of visual arts, film, theatre, music, dance and comedy. We work extensively with our local community, schools and colleges and create award-winning work for, with and by young people. In our fortieth year we have co-produced with the Sherman Theatre, Hijinx, Gagglebabble and The Other Room in Cardiff, Paines Plough, Vicky Graham Productions, HighTide, Hampstead Theatre, Bristol Old Vic, The Rose Theatre, Kingston, Headlong, Sheffield Theatres and the Orange Tree Theatre.

Over 200,000 people a year come through our doors and in 2015 Theatr Clwyd was voted the Most Welcoming Theatre in Wales.

01352 701521
www.theatrclwyd.com

HEROINE

Nessah Muthy

Acknowledgements

With eternal loving thanks to my family: Martin Mallon, Willow Mallon, Lee Parvin-Cooper, Hannah Parvin-Cooper, Carol Lacey, John Lacey, Andrew Mallon, Debra Mallon, Michael Mallon, Steven Mallon, Lana West, Tommy, Annie, Bella, Angel, Buffy, Spike and Darla.

Thanks to the incredible staff and teachers of The Beacon School who inspired me towards the arts and encouraged me to question the world: Jules Becker, Laine Bennet, Stuart Butcher and Adrian Penfold.

Thanks to my dearest friends and greatest supporters over the years: Helena Bell, Bobby Brook, Georgia Christou Dixon, Hasan Christou Dixon, Mona Goodwin, Debbie Hannan, Carissa Hope Lynch, Jen Holton, Trilby James, Helen Matravers, Fiona Skinner, Laura Turner, Nina Ward and Ria Zmitrowicz.

Thanks to those who've helped develop and given generously of their time to *Heroine*: Steven Atkinson and all at HighTide Theatre, Tamara Harvey, Bobby Brook, Abigail Gonda, Carissa Hope Lynch, Arts Council England and the Peggy Ramsay Foundation.

With extra-special thanks to the fantastic cast: Asmara Gabrielle, Maggie McCarthy, Wendy Morgan, Lucy Thackeray, Hannah Traylen and all the phenomenal actresses who've contributed to workshops/readings: Victoria Alcock, Debra Baker, Amelda Brown, Mona Goodwin, Lauren Lyle, Remmie Milner, Fiona Skinner and Ria Zmitrowicz.

N.M.

For my mum,
Elizabeth Carol Parvin-Cooper

Characters

GRACE, *mixed race, twenty-five*
WENDY, *thirty-five*
CHERYL, *fifty-four*
BEVERLEY, *sixty-eight*
SHELLEY, *twenty-one*

And Esme, two months

Setting

A community centre.

Croydon, South London.

Time

2017.

Note on Text

A dash (–) indicates an interruption.

This text went to press before the end of rehearsals and so may differ slightly from the play as performed.

Scene One

A hall.

Thick curtains, an eighties print.

At one end is a kitchen with counter.

At the other, a group of women, WENDY, CHERYL *and* BEVERLEY *finish up playing a game of bingo.* CHERYL *calls the numbers.*

CHERYL. Thirty-four, dirty whore –

   GRACE *enters. She stands alone for a second and takes in the room.*

BEVERLEY (*chanting*). Full house! Full house! Full house, full house, full house, full hoooooouse! Full hoooooouse!

   WENDY *approaches* GRACE.

WENDY. You came!

GRACE. Hi –

WENDY. Welcome!

GRACE. Thanks –

WENDY. You alright?

GRACE. Yeah –

WENDY. Missed out on the bingo –

GRACE. Oh, it's alright –

WENDY. Cheryl –

CHERYL. Alright –

   GRACE *nods to* CHERYL.

WENDY. – and Bev –

BEVERLEY. Oh, hello –

> GRACE *nods to* BEVERLEY.

> I thought it might be Linda…?

CHERYL. Linda don't come no more –

BEVERLEY. Oh…?

WENDY (*to* CHERYL). This is the girl I was telling you about…

CHERYL. Oh…?

WENDY. Yeah…

CHERYL. Actually – [turnt up]

WENDY. Yeah –

CHERYL. Hello…

GRACE. Hi –

CHERYL. Hi… Sit yourself down, eh?

GRACE. Nah, s'alright –

BEVERLEY. Another game?

WENDY. Let's do the tea and cake now –

CHERYL. Yeah –

BEVERLEY. Oh, alright then –

GRACE. I don't want anyone to go to any trouble…

CHERYL. It's no trouble, no trouble at all… (*To* BEVERLEY.) I'll get the cakes; you get the kettle on –

BEVERLEY. Alright –

WENDY. Cheers –

> *As they travel off:*

BEVERLEY. Who is she…?

CHERYL. You know…

> BEVERLEY *enters the kitchen and* CHERYL *exits the community centre.*

GRACE. Still smells exactly the same...

WENDY. Does it?

GRACE. Yeah... Panda Pops and Play-Doh and old lady...

WENDY. Well, that's all still here in the cupboards, not the old ladies acourse... we let them out... It's nothing special... but it's our nothing special... you know it's out for tender?

GRACE. Yeah –

WENDY. Think they can Boxpark it up... like everything else round here... Ain't happening... not on our watch... Introduce yourself properly in a minute, eh?

GRACE. Erm –

WENDY. Only if you like?

GRACE. Yeah –

WENDY. Or I can – ?

GRACE. No, no that's okay –

WENDY. Great. Great.

GRACE. Just came to pop me head in really –

WENDY. Oh – ?

GRACE. Yeah –

WENDY. Too much, the articles I sent – ?

GRACE. No –

WENDY. Bugger it –

GRACE. I just –

WENDY. Don't, you don't have to go –

GRACE. I better –

WENDY. One cuppa –

GRACE. You're alright –

WENDY. One cake...? Go on...

GRACE. The thing is… erm… am I? I dunno… if this is… for me?

WENDY. What you talking about?! It's like I told you, everyone is welcome –

GRACE. Right…

WENDY. Sit down, go on, sit down –

Beat.

Might be tricky –

GRACE. Sorry?

WENDY. To introduce ya, because we only met that once –

GRACE. Right –

WENDY. Ain't a lot on your Facebook –

GRACE. Nah it's crap, innit?

WENDY. Well, I wouldn't go that far, you got that photo of a cat –

GRACE. Nah, I meant Facebook in general –

WENDY. Oh right, yeah. Crap. Except when you wanna find people. Found ya!

GRACE. Yeah –

WENDY. I was thinking the plan with new people should be that they say a bit about themselves. 'I'm such and such and I love a bit of Bowie, I love baking, I'm into sexualised taxidermy – '

GRACE. What?

WENDY. What?

GRACE. What did you just say?

WENDY. What?!

Beat.

I'm just G-ing ya up – !

GRACE *laughs, awkward.*

I don't even know what that is?! What is it?! Do you?!
I don't?! Bants! Bants! We like bants, us lot –

GRACE. Right...

WENDY. How's your hand?

GRACE. Yeah –

WENDY. Nasty, eh?

GRACE. Sore –

WENDY. Stitches?

GRACE. Nah –

WENDY. You get to the hospital?

GRACE. Nah –

WENDY. Shoulda taken ya –

GRACE. Pretty mental, weren't I?

WENDY. Pretty much –

GRACE. Would've been a waste of your time, your petrol –

WENDY. Not a waste. We've got to stick together. We listen
and we stick together –

GRACE. Okay –

WENDY. Does that sound like a cult?

GRACE. Erm –

WENDY. Because that's not, this isn't, that's not what this is –

GRACE. Cool, good to know –

WENDY. And Cheryl's only locked the doors because we have
to –

GRACE. The doors – ?

WENDY. Because it's easier that way –

GRACE. Those doors – ?

WENDY. Because otherwise people try and leave before we say
so –

GRACE. Oh…

WENDY. I'm joking, I'm having you on –

WENDY *laughs*.

GRACE. Oh –

WENDY. Your face –

GRACE. Okay…

GRACE *laughs, awkward*.

WENDY. Sorry, I shouldn't have. Bugger, properly scared ya, ain't I? Tea? The tea's not got the drugs in. What's wrong with me?! Shit… Please don't leave –

GRACE. Erm –

WENDY. Shit that sounds worse –

GRACE. Erm –

WENDY. Shall we start again? Hi, I'm normal; I'm a normal human being.

Silence.

GRACE *laughs*.

GRACE. You're funny.

WENDY *laughs*.

Awkward as, but funny.

WENDY. I'm sorry –

GRACE. It's okay –

WENDY. Oh God –

GRACE. S'alright –

WENDY. Me nerves. I always get so nervous before meetings. Sorry –

GRACE. Weren't nervous when I first met you –

WENDY. No. But here, here, I want to make sure we're serving everyone right, that everyone feels like they have a voice, because they do.

GRACE. I never thanked you… for helping me, that day, it meant, something… thank you –

WENDY. No problem… you're welcome…

BEVERLEY (*from the kitchen, to* GRACE). Milk, sugar?

GRACE. Erm, no tea for me thanks –

BEVERLEY. Oh…

CHERYL *approaches* GRACE *and* WENDY *with two plates of sliced-up cakes.*

CHERYL. Here we go… that's carrot cake and that's chocolate, have a bit of both if you like – ?

GRACE. Cheers –

BEVERLEY. Save some for me –

WENDY. How those teas coming along?

BEVERLEY. Kettle playing up again, I've given it a whack –

WENDY. Let's get started anyway. Notices: Thanks, Cheryl, for making the cakes again!

CHERYL. No worries! Enjoy! Fill your boots!

The women cheer.

WENDY. Right, we need to make our Facebook, and all our social media in fact, much more active, let people know we're here, so I was thinking of giving you the password, Cheryl, you up for posting articles and photos – ?

CHERYL. Sure, why not, I'll give it a go –

WENDY. That's great, thanks, Cheryl –

BEVERLEY (*from the kitchen*). And me –

WENDY. You haven't got a computer – ?

BEVERLEY (*from the kitchen*). No –

WENDY. So what you on about – ?!

BEVERLEY (*from the kitchen*). I got an iPad though –

WENDY. Since when?

BEVERLEY (*from the kitchen*). For the kids. '4Gs Bev' you'll be calling me soon enough. You show me how and I'll do your activity for you –

The women 'Whoo!'

WENDY. Secondly, we gotta divide up the leaflets; everything is on there, like we discussed, our mission statement –

WENDY *pulls out leaflets and a map with coloured stickers.*

And these are the streets we wanna hit. Bev, you're orange stickers; Cheryl, you're red and I'm green –

BEVERLEY (*from the kitchen*). I love orange, me –

WENDY. I know, I know you do. And what else do you love, Bev –

BEVERLEY *comes back with the teas and hands them out.*

BEVERLEY. Saveloys –

WENDY. No –

BEVERLEY. Frankfurters –

WENDY. Nope –

BEVERLEY. Salami –

WENDY. No, no, a T-shirt – !

BEVERLEY. Oh yeah –

WENDY. I've got them all printed for us –

The women cheer.

Great. Well, get your dosh out because they're £13.50 each.

The women grumble.

Freedom-fighting comes at a price! And that price is £13.50 so shut up and cough up, I can't pay for everything –

CHERYL. How many you got there?

WENDY. Bought in bulk, hopefully sell a few after the march. (*To* GRACE.) Our first, silent march, through the high street, this Saturday, obviously we'd absolutely love you to join us, no pressure, but we'd love it. Which leads me on to… our visitor and hopefully new member... Grace... Grace, do you want to tell us a bit about yourself...

GRACE. Erm... nah... I'm... I'm not really used to these kind of things –

WENDY. Come on...

GRACE. I don't think this is for me –

WENDY. That's a shame... that's a real shame.

GRACE. I just... er... I don't think it's for me, or I'm for you, or –

WENDY. You are welcome; she was in the army. Tell them what you done –

GRACE. IED sweeper, Afghan –

CHERYL. Was ya – ?

WENDY. Yeah...

BEVERLEY. Well, that's something, innit...

The women clap.

GRACE. Nah, you don't need to do that...

Beat.

Thanks... but erm... the thing is –

WENDY. Now she's a postie, cos they won't let her back –

The women tut.

GRACE. Well, I got a heart condition –

WENDY. Maybe you could tell us a bit about why you came...

GRACE. Why I came?

WENDY. Yeah...

GRACE. I came, because, I met you –

WENDY. Yes –

GRACE. I might as well be honest; I'd just punched a wall –

BEVERLEY. Oh...?

WENDY. Fella at the post office suspended her –

GRACE (*to* WENDY). And well... you was the only one that stopped and helped. And you was nice to me...

BEVERLEY. She's lovely, our Wend...

GRACE. Yeah...

Beat.

I came because, erm...

Beat.

I don't know... I'm struggling...

Beat.

CHERYL. It's okay... You're alright, love...

GRACE. Sorry...

CHERYL. Take your time...

GRACE. I wanna make a change... make a difference...

WENDY. That's right –

GRACE. And I thought someone might listen... and I might not be judged...

WENDY. Good girl. Good girl...

Scene Two

GRACE *waits alone.*

After a moment, BEVERLEY *enters.*

BEVERLEY. Oh... hello...?

GRACE. Hi –

BEVERLEY. You came back?

GRACE. Erm –

BEVERLEY. How come? You never showed for the march?

GRACE. Seemed a bit pointless –

BEVERLEY. Oh? We ain't for everyone, when we get heated, when we get passionate –

GRACE. That's erm, that's the thing though, you lot got all this passion. But staying silent, what's that about?

BEVERLEY. What do you mean?

GRACE. Didn't seem like it was gonna do anything? Did it?

BEVERLEY. Erm, well... no, as it happens... You got French Fancies in that bag?

GRACE. Erm –

BEVERLEY. You gonna lay them out...?

GRACE. I dunno –

BEVERLEY. Forgot to cook meself any dinner, stupid idiot, I am, done the grandkids but not meself, what an idiot, eh? Gotta make sure their brains keep growing. They gotta know how to fight, be strong enough, when they have to...

GRACE. Yeah...

BEVERLEY *eyes the bag.*

You want one of these now?

BEVERLEY. Nah, nah –

GRACE. You sure?

BEVERLEY. Better wait –

GRACE. Go on…

BEVERLEY. Oh no, I didn't mean –

GRACE. I've opened them now…

> GRACE *hands* BEVERLEY *a cake.*

> BEVERLEY *eats the cake ravenously.*

BEVERLEY. Thank you. Thank you very much.

GRACE. Why don't you take the lot, eh?

BEVERLEY. Oh no I can't do that –

GRACE. For your grandkids? For later…?

BEVERLEY. But –

GRACE. I won't tell if you don't –

BEVERLEY. They'll love these, proper treat, eh?

GRACE. Are they with you permanent, your grandkids?

BEVERLEY. For a while –

GRACE. That's erm, that's very good of ya –

BEVERLEY. Is what it is… they're good girls… hard work… but good girls. They had a free tap trial in here yesterday… can't afford to bring them back… dunno if I should have given them a taste… like animals smelling the blood… but I used to love it at school… good toes, naughty toes, good toes, naughty toes… Music and movement, everything else I went in a brown study for…

GRACE. Who's got them now?

BEVERLEY. Oh, me neighbour. It's nice to have a bit of a break to be honest… ain't a lot I can do with them really, used to take them to the park, but I don't like staying out too late and it gets proper dark this time of year… can't see nothing, can't see who might be coming your way…

GRACE. No…

BEVERLEY. I'm lucky I got good friends. Cheryl, she's a sweetheart, she's knitted the kids hats and scarves... lived down the road from me, thirty, knocking on thirty-five years –

GRACE. Lovely –

BEVERLEY. And Wendy she sometimes wraps the leftovers up for me here... because I can't always get in the foodbank... well... cos it's rammed, rammed with liquorice allsorts... and she's helping me with interview technique, I got one tomorrow actually, dinner lady, oh 'midday supervisor'.

Beat.

What you looking at me like that for? What, I'm twenty-five?! Case of having to, love...

GRACE. Yeah –

BEVERLEY. We're all so packed in on the estate, I can't breathe and sometimes it feels like I can't even breathe in the park...

GRACE. Of course –

BEVERLEY. And I shouldn't be scared –

GRACE. It's disgusting –

BEVERLEY. But I am scared... for myself... for my grandkids... They're just little girls... The politicians, the papers, they won't tell ya, but I know, I know what goes on... If we don't look out for each other, no one will –

GRACE. That's right... we have to –

BEVERLEY. Where are you from?

GRACE. I'm English, but people always think I'm not, think I'm foreign I guess. Me mum was English... but it was me nana that raised me...

BEVERLEY. Oh right –

GRACE. In fact, the day after September 11th, right, this boy turned round to me in here, in youth club –

BEVERLEY. Oh –

GRACE. Over there actually –

BEVERLEY. No –

GRACE. Said, 'It was you lot that done that, weren't it?' I didn't know what to say because I was too busy realising that people don't get me –

BEVERLEY. You've ended up being a victim of it an' all, people thinking wrong things about ya? Born and bred you are...

GRACE. In me heart yeah, it's what I went and fought for, weren't it...?

BEVERLEY. Yeah, course you did –

GRACE. Bev, I'll walk you home later if you like?

BEVERLEY. Would ya? That'd be lovely –

GRACE. Ain't nothing to be scared of, we stick together –

CHERYL *enters*.

CHERYL (*to* BEVERLEY). Hello...

BEVERLEY. Hello –

CHERYL (*to* GRACE). Oh... hello...

GRACE. Alright?

CHERYL. How are ya? How'd the job go?

GRACE. Yeah... dead in the water...

BEVERLEY. Oh no, you never said?

CHERYL. Sorry... sorry to hear that...

GRACE. Weren't for me...

WENDY *enters carrying a flipchart*.

WENDY. Can somebody bloody help me, Cheryl – ?

CHERYL *assists* WENDY.

CHERYL. Grace came back, Wend...

WENDY (*to* GRACE). So I see...

    GRACE *nods*.

    You missed Saturday –

GRACE. Yeah, sorry –

WENDY. We were counting on you –

CHERYL. She lost her job –

WENDY. Well, I'm sorry, but –

BEVERLEY. Shall I get the bingo cards out?

WENDY. No we're skipping bingo tonight –

BEVERLEY. But it's my turn to call –

WENDY. Not tonight, love. It's much worse than we could
    have ever imagined... I can't even...

CHERYL. What is it?

WENDY. They've sold this place to the Saudis.

CHERYL. What?!

WENDY. It's gonna be a Saudi-funded Islamic Centre to
    promote the Wahabi version of Islam –

BEVERLEY. What does that mean?

WENDY. It's what ISIS follow, Bev, extremism, terrorist
    breeding ground right here, right in our home –

    Silence.

CHERYL. They can't –

WENDY. They can and they will –

BEVERLEY. It's evil... it's pure evil is what it is...

WENDY. There's no point complaining. We are gonna stop it.
    We need to get brainstorming –

BEVERLEY. Can't say that – !

WENDY. What?

BEVERLEY. 'Brainstorming – '

WENDY. Why?!

BEVERLEY. Offensive to the epileptics. 'Thought shower' –

WENDY. Anyway. A petition and a silent march –

GRACE. Fuck's sake – !

WENDY. Oh hello?! What you got then, Grace?

GRACE. Nobody's hearing ya, how is silence gonna save this place?

WENDY. It's peaceful… it's respectful… it's what we stand for…

GRACE. You can't just be respectful though, you gotta be heard –

CHERYL. She's right –

GRACE. We need to do something where people have to take notice –

WENDY. Okay, like what?

GRACE. We gotta go to the council, in the offices get to the people that have approved this and stand there and make a scene until they listen –

CHERYL. I like that –

BEVERLEY. Me too, I can film it on me iPad, get it on the Facebook –

GRACE. Give people something to watch –

BEVERLEY. Yeah –

WENDY. We have to be careful, very careful –

CHERYL. They ain't being careful though, are they, Wend?

WENDY. No…

CHERYL. It's like it's now or never, innit? (*To* GRACE.) When you thinking?

GRACE. Soon as, couple of days?

CHERYL. Yeah – !

GRACE. Shall I put it on the flipchart?

WENDY. We'd have to think about it all, properly, go through step by step –

GRACE. Acourse –

WENDY. Get banners –

GRACE. Okay –

WENDY. Do speeches –

GRACE. No problem –

WENDY *throws* GRACE *a pen.*

WENDY. Go on then, Grace, you write –

GRACE *half-smiles.* GRACE *stands,* GRACE *writes.*

CHERYL. What do we reckon the banners should say?

WENDY. Something simple, something clear –

BEVERLEY. 'Fuck off you cunts'?

WENDY. Something like that...

GRACE. No surrender?

WENDY. Yeah, yeah I like it –

BEVERLEY. No fucking surrender!

CHERYL. Will the banners be big enough?

BEVERLEY. Well, one of us holds 'No fucking' and the other holds 'surrender' –

CHERYL. But then those two people would have to be together and what if they accidentally stood in the wrong position? Then it's: 'surrender no fucking' –

BEVERLEY. It still works for me, Cheryl, just means people have to have a good look, use their noggin –

WENDY. I think just 'no surrender' –

BEVERLEY. It was just a suggestion –

WENDY. We need people to get the cause as quickly as possible. Nobody likes to have to think too much –

BEVERLEY. Me, I like a think, I like a good think –

WENDY. Okay, that's great. Anyway, Beverley, why don't you be on security, now obviously you can't touch them or nothing, but you could be our eyes and ears as to their whereabouts –

BEVERLEY. Don't you worry, girl, I got my charm ready… I'm like a snake when I get going… ssss…

WENDY. Fantastic –

CHERYL. You're spitting on me, Bev!

BEVERLEY. Am I?! Sorry!

CHERYL. Here! Have it back!

BEVERLEY. Oh! You dirty cow!

WENDY. Okay, okay. I'll obviously need to be the one running the whole operation… and starting the chants and that. We'll need as many people there as possible, so get the message out, but not on any open social networks… private messages only… taking these fuckers by surprise is key. And we'll need a speaker with a clear voice and –

GRACE. I'll do it. I'll speak.

Scene Three

With the exception of GRACE, *the women dance to 'Superman' by Black Lace.*

GRACE *sits and watches.*

WENDY. Can I just say... I'm proper... proper proud of you, everyone...

   CHERYL *shrills with delight.*

CHERYL. I haven't felt like this in years!

BEVERLEY. Don't let your Danny hear you talk like that!

CHERYL. Danny can't find the cutlery drawer, let alone anything else – !

   CHERYL *shrills again.*

WENDY (*to* BEVERLEY). You alright?

BEVERLEY. What'd you mean, am I alright?!

CHERYL. Body ain't what it used to be, eh, Bev?

BEVERLEY. Sod off!

CHERYL. I got some Deep Heat in me bag –

BEVERLEY. Get away with ya! Deep Heat?! Was worth it for their faces –

CHERYL. Their faces, our faces?!

BEVERLEY. Didn't see none of you lot giving it a go –

CHERYL. We was too busy with the chain, which you was meant to be part of –

BEVERLEY. Yeah, well, something just came over me –

CHERYL. Sommink came over that pillar, you mean – !

BEVERLEY. Got all them security guards distracted, didn't I?! 'Touch me again, I'm a pensioner!'

   BEVERLEY *races up to* CHERYL, *Dirty Dancing last dance/lift style.*

'Time of Your Life' me, Cherl!

CHERYL. What?! I'm only one woman!

BEVERLEY. I wasn't gonna give in –

WENDY. They were gonna call the police –

GRACE. Yeah, but we didn't even get past reception though –

CHERYL. Next time –

BEVERLEY. I would have stuck it; they don't call me thunder thighs for nothing –

CHERYL. Who calls you that then, eh?!

BEVERLEY. Never you mind! There have been callers… over the years…

WENDY *and* CHERYL *'Whoo!'*

I had at least another three and a half minutes in me –

CHERYL. Yeah, but the pillar didn't! It was soggy!

BEVERLEY. How rude!

WENDY. It don't matter, we sent a message, a clear message and people turned out for us, how many likes now?! –

BEVERLEY *pulls out her iPad.*

BEVERLEY. It's gone mental! Over a hundred! What did I tell ya… 'Hashtag Hug-a-Pillar Bev' –

WENDY. Seriously?!

CHERYL *stops dancing and approaches* GRACE.

CHERYL (*to* GRACE). Speech was amazing… my best bit…

GRACE. There weren't loads of people though, I don't know if enough people heard – ?

WENDY (*indicating the phone*). They will do on here, views keep going up and up, look –

CHERYL (*to* GRACE). You done really good, so proud of you –

WENDY. It was fucking brilliant –

BEVERLEY. Whoo-whoo! Oh…

WENDY. Bev...?

WENDY *turns the music down, the dancing stops.*

BEVERLEY. Blow me...

CHERYL. What is it?!

WENDY. Oh here... sit down...

WENDY *helps* BEVERLEY *to a chair.*

CHERYL. Shall I get the Deep Heat? I'm getting it...

BEVERLEY. Only because you insist!

CHERYL *returns and lifts up* BEVERLEY*'s top.*

Oh, you int half a good girl, Cheryl...

CHERYL. Yeah... pay me later...

BEVERLEY. I've got a lovely back, you're bloody lucky actually... to have this opportunity –

CHERYL. Shut your gob, or you'll end up with this sprayed in there!

CHERYL *sprays.*

BEVERLEY. Ooh! Thank you. Thank you very much.

BEVERLEY*'s stomach rumbles loudly.* BEVERLEY *quickly pulls down her T-shirt and laughs.*

Oh! Sorry!

CHERYL. That's about the twentieth time your stomach has rumbled like that today. (*To* WENDY.) She's not looking after herself –

BEVERLEY. Don't talk about me like I ain't here...

WENDY. We only care about ya –

BEVERLEY *sniffs and shrugs.*

Have some cakes, eh – ?

CHERYL. I think she needs something more substantial than cakes, don't you? Come on, come home with me –

BEVERLEY. No –

CHERYL. Don't be silly –

BEVERLEY. I said no, I don't want nothing –

CHERYL. You can't survive on nothing –

BEVERLEY. I have to –

CHERYL. No you don't, I'm offering –

BEVERLEY. Yeah but you ain't there all the time, are ya? I've got meself to a point and I can't –

CHERYL. What are you talking about?!

BEVERLEY. If I eat what you give me, it's gonna mess me up and I've nearly paid it off, I'm nearly sorted –

WENDY. Paid what off?

CHERYL. You done that loan, didn't ya? I told you not to –

WENDY. And me –

BEVERLEY. I had to! And anyway I got the job, didn't I, start training tomorrow. I come here not to think about it –

CHERYL. Well, you gotta be thinking about it –

BEVERLEY. Couple more weeks and I'll be paid –

CHERYL *scoffs*.

Then I can do a big food shop –

CHERYL. Couple more weeks where she don't eat?! Between the lot of us, we'll feed ya, won't we –

BEVERLEY. No –

CHERYL. Shut up –

WENDY. Of course –

BEVERLEY. I don't want it…

CHERYL. Every meal –

WENDY. We'll get a rota…

BEVERLEY. I don't wanna be a burden –

CHERYL. The kids and all, that's alright, innit, girls?

WENDY. Acourse.

CHERYL. Ain't a burden, you're our mate and it starts now, you're coming home with me... I got toad-in-the-hole –

BEVERLEY *takes* CHERYL*'s hand.*

BEVERLEY. I proper love toad-in-the-hole –

CHERYL. I know you do... Why don't you lot come an' all, eh?

WENDY. Oh lovely yeah, but I might just need a hand stashing stuff away. Is that alright, Grace?

GRACE. Yeah –

WENDY. Cheers –

CHERYL (*to* BEVERLEY). Get your bag out the cupboard then, girl...

CHERYL *gets her own bag out of the cupboard, followed by* BEVERLEY.

See you in a bit...

WENDY. Won't be long –

BEVERLEY. See ya –

CHERYL *and* BEVERLEY *exit.*

WENDY *and* GRACE *begin to fold the banners neatly into the cupboard.*

GRACE. She'll be alright, eh?

WENDY. Yeah, acourse. We'll look after her... Really, *really,* something today –

GRACE. We didn't get far enough in though; we didn't get to the actual people that need to hear it –

WENDY. It's a really good start, it came from here – (*Her heart.*) it was true... What was that bit? 'I, er, I fought for this country, for freedom, for peace... for...' I filmed it...

WENDY *looks for her phone but instead* GRACE *recites...*

GRACE. I went to fight for hope I, I wasn't ready to come home, but… I've realised the war is raging at home and it ain't about race, it's about values. We have the right to feel safe on our streets, people should walk freely, women and children should live and work and play without violence… things are out of control… and this… this… Islamic Centre… what they're planning on building in the heart of our community will become a place of pure hate… built with Saudi money. And that will kill us. We need to take back control, not politicians, not the police, us, the people, we are the power…

WENDY. There's something I should tell you –

GRACE. Yeah?

WENDY. The other girls know… but I didn't wanna scare ya off.

GRACE. Scare me how?

WENDY. Although today was peaceful we still got to keep our wits about us –

GRACE. Right, so what's our next move – ?

WENDY. Might be some retaliation…

GRACE. I know –

WENDY. No, you don't know –

Beat.

I wanna tell ya, because I wanna keep you safe…

GRACE. Okay…

WENDY. Few years back. I got moved away from here. Relocated. Officially. Weren't safe for me and my family. I got me head kicked in…

WENDY *lifts up her hair.*

GRACE. Jesus…

WENDY. Metal plate in there now…

GRACE. Fuck…

WENDY. Yeah…

GRACE. EDL?

WENDY. What?

GRACE. From your EDL days?

Beat.

WENDY. Must have scratched deep to find that, eh?

GRACE. I had a good scratch –

WENDY. It ain't what you think –

GRACE. No – ?

WENDY. It ain't –

GRACE. Oh right –

WENDY. You're adding two and two and getting five...

Beat.

Alright, hands up, I was in it at the beginning, but it was when there was nothing else... or I hadn't thought of nothing else... I had this cousin who was being used as... well, 'moist white meat' is what they called her... a grooming gang... until I decided no, no you ain't gonna be called that no more... what you're gonna do is fight...

Beat.

Labour didn't do anything... the Tories didn't either... even UKIP and the BNP didn't do enough... so street-protesting with the EDL was our only way... and we became like a family I suppose... my little Croydon Division...

Beat.

But the trouble with families is the same trouble with street-protesting, you can't control them and you don't know who you're gonna become because of who you're surrounded by... We were too pissed and we were too violent... no one listened and nothing was changing. I realised I'd let meself get so angry... so hateful... that I'd forgotten, why I wanted to do this in the first place... that I wanted to help...

Beat.

So I left... but erm, before I could even think about what that meant, one night... Antifa... you heard of Antifa – ?

GRACE. No –

WENDY. They counter-demo everything, they can get nasty, really fucking nasty... and erm... a group of them, of men... jumped me... pushed me to the ground and screamed in my face: 'What you gonna do now, you racist?' I screamed back at them: 'I am not racist!' So then one of them... stood on my head... literally and he said: 'You're gonna fucking stop!' I didn't have anything to lose... so I just screamed back, as loud as I fucking could: 'No!'

Beat.

Then he booted me... and I woke up in hospital three weeks later...

Beat.

And... no... before you ask, they didn't get convicted... not enough evidence...

WENDY *sniggers.*

Beat.

Police moved us... in the end... can you believe that? Said it was just safer that way. Away with her, no regard for the fact that this was my home. But, I couldn't stand it. So I came back... got into the heart of the community and built this group. Don't matter what colour you are, what race, what religion, it's for all women that want the hate to stop and women that want a better way to be heard...

Beat.

Better an ex-EDL-er than a new one...

Beat.

So in fact – (*Indicating her head.*) not EDL days, not at all, but if you wanna leave –

GRACE. I don't want to leave. I wouldn't be here otherwise, would I...?

WENDY. No... no... I guess not...

GRACE. Cheers for telling me though.

WENDY. Right...

Beat.

The last thing I'd want is for anything to happen to ya...

GRACE. Thank you, I appreciate that.

WENDY. I'm not a racist –

GRACE. I know –

WENDY. I'm not. I am a counter-jihadist, not a Muslim-hater just for the sake of hating. I don't hate all Muslims, far from it... there are amazing Muslims... l know there's a distinction and I try to make sure everyone who walks through that door knows it too... I've looked at the Qur'ān, I've studied it and I've studied Wahhabism... there's a difference, Wahhabism is a hateful, intolerant evil reading of Islam... not for round here... not anywhere... but if this council, the bloody government can't see it, won't ban this Saudi-money Islamic Centre then –

GRACE. We have to find a way ourselves...

WENDY. For everybody... This time it's different, it feels different, we've got a strategy and a plan and you're here, aren't ya?

GRACE. Yeah –

WENDY. Because I'd really like it if you were to take over here one day, Grace. I can see how that might be better for all of us –

GRACE. I gotcha...

WENDY *nods.*

So what we gonna do next...?

WENDY. You tell me, eh...?

GRACE. All they're doing is making mutineers out of us women...

WENDY. Yeah… yeah… I like that… mutineers…

GRACE. My nana, she would always tell me, don't ever let yourself be scared, girl, instead, fucking roar…

GRACE *roars*.

WENDY *roars*.

GRACE *and* WENDY *roar together*.

WENDY *and* GRACE *laugh together*.

A woman, SHELLEY, *enters*.

SHELLEY. Right fucking shithole this place –

WENDY. Hello – ?

SHELLEY. I wanna speak to her –

WENDY. Can I help?

SHELLEY. Oh, piss off –

WENDY. Piss off yourself, out – !

SHELLEY. Grace –

GRACE. It's alright. I'll sort it, you get off to Cheryl's –

WENDY. I don't think so –

GRACE. I'll sort it –

WENDY. You know her?

GRACE. It's all good; I promise ya, go on – ?

WENDY. I'll wait in the car, shall I, the car that's just out there –

GRACE. Yeah, it's fine, don't worry, go on –

WENDY *nods and exits*.

Where's Esme?

SHELLEY. She's fine. Can't get you on the phone. I been at your flat, knocking every day –

GRACE. Well, we don't do that. We agreed. We have an arrangement –

SHELLEY. I been at the delivery office, said you went mental, said you got sacked – ?! I thought you were sorting yourself out – ?

GRACE. When I get something else, I'll backdate the payments –

SHELLEY. I been trying to square it all in me head because then, then I see ya, see ya on Facebook tagged at this place, you know what this is, right?

GRACE. It's not; it's not what you think –

SHELLEY. I seen your video…

GRACE. And?

SHELLEY. Your speech…

GRACE. I'm trying to help –

SHELLEY. Right…

GRACE. Women –

SHELLEY. Yeah –

GRACE. The community –

SHELLEY. I couldn't give a fuck really –

GRACE. A family, a unit, coming together, it's not what you think –

SHELLEY *snorts*.

SHELLEY. What about your own family?!

GRACE. Maybe bigger, than that, for the country –

SHELLEY. What about *your* own?! I'm struggling… I'm trying to hold down three jobs… I have to hide her in the corner whilst I scrub some cunt's third en suite and make sure she don't projectile vomit on their Victorian enamel… or… breathe in the bleach… I'm trying to do right by her… I'm trying to be there for her… but I'm so tired… I'm worried I ain't got the time for the love… to love her…

GRACE. I know what you're doing, self-preservation, not getting too close, because you think one day… I'll take

her... but I'm telling you now... I ain't coming for her...
So love her... don't stop loving her...

SHELLEY. I don't want to have to put her in care...

GRACE. Don't you dare. You promised me...

SHELLEY. I won't, I wouldn't... but...

GRACE (*in close to* SHELLEY). I can't even look at her...
Trust me, I done the right thing... I done the *right* thing...
Maybe you wouldn't understand... maybe it's because
you're not a mother... an actual one...

Scene Four

GRACE *sits on the kitchen counter.*

BEVERLEY *and* CHERYL *sit around the table.*

WENDY *enters.*

WENDY. You seen this?

　WENDY *chucks a local newspaper on the table.*

CHERYL. Oh yeah, we've seen it alright, they've smeared us –

BEVERLEY. In shit –

CHERYL. Think we're a load of 'far-right terrorists'! 'Ignorant'
I ain't ignorant...

GRACE. None of us are –

WENDY. It's disgraceful –

BEVERLEY. Some arsehole, keeps messaging me quotes from
the Bible –

WENDY. What?!

BEVERLEY. Pretending they're from the Qur'ān, asking me,
what do I think about them...?

GRACE. What'd you say?

BEVERLEY. I said, why are you sending me quotes from the Bible?!

GRACE. Good on ya –

BEVERLEY. We couldn't get served down the chippy. Ain't gonna serve 'racist Islamaphobes' –

WENDY. I'm sorry –

CHERYL. I was nearly bloody arrested trying to defend us –

BEVERLEY. Weren't even Mrs Chippy herself, it was some kind of mob in the queue, real nasty, in front of the kids –

CHERYL. And it says, they're still going ahead with selling this place...

WENDY. I know –

CHERYL. So?!

WENDY. I'm as gutted as you lot, alright?! I got the hall manager on my back, no one gets it, I've had to tell her we're sticking to our bingo and that's it –

GRACE. We're not doing that though, are we?

WENDY. We were clear in our message, and we weren't violent... people watched the video, three hundred watched –

CHERYL. Well, they ain't here, are they...?!

WENDY. Fuck's sake –

GRACE. So what are we doing? Wend?! If we aren't gonna have actual effects in real terms...?

BEVERLEY. It was your idea, weren't it? All this...?

GRACE. Yeah, alright, it was... To be honest, I don't get it at all, it ain't even about race, it's about a religion. They ain't read the Qur'ān, they ain't got the faintest idea about Wahhabism, how it's gonna be preached here, that, that hate is gonna be here in the heart of our community –

BEVERLEY. Don't want to listen to me, I'm 'offensive', apparently –

GRACE. But offended never killed no one, offended never ran
a van into someone or blew them up... Islamaphobe?!
Totally nonsensical... it is *not* extreme to fear that someone
might stab you... Is it?

CHERYL. No, acourse not –

GRACE. We're the ones trying to protect them, their families,
their kids. There's been a terrorist attack somewhere in the
world every week for months... we've been at war since
2001 and no fucker realises it or wants to –

CHERYL. Yeah, I hear ya. It's because we're asking them to
look and listen and if they do that, they'll have to do
something about it –

GRACE. But we've gotta find a way, for our community, our
country and our kids, we're the only ones who see it like it
is... You go back out there and you say to them: 'I am not
a racist, I'm a mutineer...'

CHERYL. Yeah –

GRACE. Isn't that right, Wend?

WENDY. Erm... yeah...

BEVERLEY. In a way, it's not even the Muslims that is the
problem...

WENDY. Radical, radical Muslims –

BEVERLEY. Yes, yes, the radical ones, they're not the problem –

CHERYL. What are you talking about? You been on the
Moonshine?!

BEVERLEY. It's the white posh liberals, int it? I been doing my
training up the school, the teachers, the staff and even the
inclusion officer is more worried about being called a racist
than dealing with any actual, proper racism... And the
yummy mummies in the playground, they won't even say the
word... Muslim... they're scared of it... just the word...

GRACE. You're absolutely on the fucking money, Bev... we
need to think differently...

BEVERLEY. How though? Even you're not enough proof...
They left you out, didn't they... you're only on our Facebook
page... your speech, your face... ain't in the paper –

GRACE. That's right and that's why I've got an idea... what if
I dressed up as a Muslim... wore a burqa... I start gentle, but
then I start to read out some of things that the hate preachers
have said and we see how long these liberals... can hack it
for... if they can stomach it... see if some even agree to that...
and then I rip off the burqa... and I reveal our T-shirt... and
I shame them about what they've just allowed themselves to
swallow...

BEVERLEY. That's a plan and a half, innit, eh?

CHERYL. I think it's fucking amazing –

GRACE. It's just an idea –

BEVERLEY. No, no, I think it's clever –

CHERYL. So what would you say exactly?

GRACE. Nothing dodgy, just exactly what's there... direct
quotes... truth... stuff they don't look at, stuff what Wend
sent us...

BEVERLEY. What you thinking eh, Wend? Up the council?

GRACE. No actually, there's a demo, up London, I wanna do it
there –

CHERYL. I could nick Danny's cab if you like, saves on train
fares –

GRACE. Yes, Cherl – !

WENDY. What demo?

GRACE. UK Hate, Hate –

WENDY. Nah –

GRACE. Why not?

WENDY. EDL will be there –

GRACE. So –

WENDY. *We're* not EDL –

GRACE. We won't have anything to do with them; we'll fly our own banner. Mutineer Women, yeah – ?

WENDY. I don't know – ?

GRACE. We'll be distinct; get new T-shirts printed –

WENDY. It's never that simple and –

GRACE. This is about freedom of speech, freedom of assembly... and it just so happens that we might give saving this place a fighting chance... if we can get people to listen about why we don't want radical Islam at all –

WENDY. These demos are big – how do you think you're gonna be heard? Anyway, I don't want to just piggyback on something else –

GRACE. It's not piggybacking. I'll put myself right at the centre... I'm gonna go right in the middle of Antifa –

BEVERLEY. Who?

WENDY. Anti-Fascists –

GRACE. That's who we're talking about, Bev, the white posh liberals that scream 'racist': white privilege. They're like the organised ones, the ones that turn up and counter-demo –

WENDY. It's not just the white posh liberals you have to worry about, there's loads of different people in it with them, they say they're Anti-Fascist, but they can get proper violent –

GRACE. I can handle violence –

WENDY. Yeah but can everyone else?

GRACE. I'll make sure no one gets hurt. I'll get us into the right part of Antifa, it'll be alright. (*To* CHERYL *and* BEVERLEY.) There's gonna be a lot of people there, proper big news crews –

CHERYL. Sounds like it's our chance to be properly heard, Wend?

BEVERLEY. When is it?

GRACE. Next week –

CHERYL. That's plenty of prep time –

WENDY (*to* CHERYL *and* BEVERLEY). Go and get the flipchart out me car, will ya – ?

CHERYL. Come on, Bev –

BEVERLEY. What?! Me as well?!

WENDY (*to* BEVERLEY). Go on, girl –

BEVERLEY *and* CHERYL *exit.*

GRACE. What's the deal with Cheryl?

WENDY. What about her?

GRACE. Well, she gets all excited, she makes cake and that, but what is she?

WENDY. She's one of you lot –

GRACE. What's that – ?

WENDY. Army. Lost her daughter.

GRACE. Oh…

WENDY. Yeah…

Beat.

You're sure you wanna go through with this?

GRACE. What?

WENDY. If you wanna back out now's the time –

GRACE. Why would I do that?

WENDY. Because it's a big thing. Ain't marching up the council, ain't small fry.

GRACE. I get that –

WENDY. It's big.

Beat.

'Death threats to family' big…

GRACE. Yeah –

WENDY. You can't rely on no one to protect you...

GRACE. You lot – ?

WENDY. I meant the state, the police... You ready for that?

GRACE. Yes –

WENDY. Your family ready for that?

Beat.

It might be something you wanna go and have a think about. Before you get our ladies' hopes up...

GRACE. I'm here, aren't I? I said I'll do it... so I'll do it.

Beat.

Do *you* not want me to do it? Is that what you're getting at – ?

WENDY. I don't know, things can get out of hand, I wanna keep everyone safe.

GRACE. Don't seem to know if you wanna win or if you wanna lose, Wend?

Beat.

WENDY. So what about them – ?

GRACE. Who – ?

WENDY. Your family – ?

GRACE. I ain't got one of those...

WENDY. Right –

GRACE. Nah... What?

WENDY. Everyone's got a family...

GRACE. Have they?

WENDY. Yeah –

GRACE. No... no one...

WENDY *nods*.

WENDY. That girl, the other day... who was she then...?

Beat.

Looked pretty upset about something...?

Beat.

This ain't the group to tell lies... have secrets... she'd found you here...

GRACE. She's no one...

WENDY. Alright... alright, fine... maybe you tell me when you're ready –

GRACE. There's nothing to tell...

WENDY. Mmm-hmm.

Beat.

But you do know her?

Beat.

GRACE. Sister...

WENDY. Right...

GRACE. Half...

WENDY. Right...

GRACE. Yeah...

WENDY. What did she want?

GRACE. It was about my daughter –

WENDY. You do have something to care for then?

GRACE. I don't care for her –

WENDY. Legally or...?

GRACE. It's just better if she's away from me...

WENDY. What's that supposed to mean?

GRACE. Nothing –

WENDY. Now you're confusing me... even worrying me a little bit –

GRACE. It ain't what you think –

WENDY. What am I thinking?

GRACE. I dunno, I ain't done nothing… Just the way things worked out –

WENDY. So your sister has her –

GRACE. Yeah, I did the right thing… the responsible thing –

WENDY. The dad – ?

GRACE. Jesus Christ! What is this, eh?! An officer. Married.

Beat.

So there you go… now what?

Beat.

You were floundering a bit out there, Wend, you were losing them, I came in, offered a solution… and that's okay…

WENDY. That's exactly what you did…

GRACE. Listen, Wend, I like you. And I believe in what you are and what you say… I just wanna be a part of it… genuinely… in my heart… I wanna see this work… make a change…

WENDY. What you doing this for then? If it ain't for your family…?

GRACE. For the world, Wend… for all of humanity… what are you doing it for?

WENDY. I'm doing it for the community, for women, but er, truth be told, I just want my girls to grow up safe…

Scene Five

GRACE *unwraps some blank banner material, gets tangled,* CHERYL *assists.*

CHERYL. Here, come here…

GRACE. She's a liability –

CHERYL. We'll sort it –

GRACE. If I say I'm gonna do something, I do it –

CHERYL. It won't take long… 'No surrender?'

GRACE. 'No fucking surrender.'

CHERYL. No fucking problem –

GRACE. Where's Bev?!

CHERYL. I'm sure she's on her way, don't worry –

GRACE. I just want everything to go to plan –

CHERYL. Acourse you do, we all do –

GRACE. Can't have you holding three peoples' banners – !

CHERYL. She'll be here –

GRACE. I planned it all out… to the second…

CHERYL. I know, you're very good, very organised. What you learnt in the army?

GRACE. Yeah…

CHERYL. Acourse…

  CHERYL *paints.*

GRACE. Your daughter… she was in Afghan…?

CHERYL. That's right…

  Beat.

  What erm… You don't have to tell me… I just sometimes… get to wondering… What was it like…?

GRACE. It's hard to explain –

CHERYL. Bet your family is just glad you're home...

GRACE. I don't know... you make it your home...

CHERYL. Right... right... can I erm, can I show you something, Grace?

CHERYL holds her phone directly in GRACE's face.

That's my girl... Elizabeth, Liz.

Beat.

My Liz was a medic, a nurse, a combat medical technician, I mean –

GRACE. Good people, them. On patrol, I'd be out front with the Vallon, everyone behind relying on me to be right. The medic right at the rear, vital –

CHERYL. Do you think you ever saw her...?

GRACE. I don't think so...

CHERYL. Yeah, acourse not, silly –

GRACE. She – ?

Beat.

CHERYL. Yeah...

Beat.

Both her legs blown off.

GRACE. Shit.

Beat.

CHERYL. You're right, shit is what it is. She was only trying to help someone, soldier, bleeding out, he was alright, he survived...

Beat.

Bastards. Bloody, fucking bastards. Sorry.

GRACE. S'alright –

CHERYL. Can't talk like this anywhere else but when I get here, I can say it, I can release it.

Beat.

I done counselling... but you're meant to be able to say whatever you want in there and you know... sometimes, they look at me like I'm... a... and I ain't... I'm just a mother...

Beat.

Well no...

Beat.

Not any more... but well... there ain't no word for that, is there... when you ain't one no more...

Beat.

She done good. She done good by me, by her dad and by this country –

GRACE. You must be very proud –

CHERYL. I am so proud of her. My baby.

Beat.

She had beautiful little legs... a kicker right from the start, right from when she was in here –

Beat.

I held her when she took her first breath.

Beat.

And you know where she was when she took her last?

Beat.

A sandy, shitty, bloody hole...

Beat.

I'll never ever forgive them –

GRACE. No –

CHERYL. Not the MOD, not Blair or them, bloody fucking bastard them –

Beat.

I come here to speak for her and I come here to see her, does that sound strange? See her spirit, her fight and for a split second...

Beat.

She's alive... do you know what I mean...?

GRACE. Yeah I think I do...

GRACE *holds out her hand.*

I'm so sorry –

CHERYL. Don't. I don't want pity –

GRACE. No, no –

CHERYL. What can I do with that, eh? I want to do something –

GRACE. Alright, alright –

CHERYL. I'm not religious or superstitious or whatever, but I think you was meant to come here, for yourself, for me... for us all...

GRACE *smiles.*

BEVERLEY *enters.*

BEVERLEY. Suspended –

CHERYL. You what, love?

BEVERLEY. From work... They saw all the stuff in the papers and Facebook, called me in to the headmistress' office...

BEVERLEY *hands* CHERYL *a letter.*

CHERYL (*reading*). 'Gross misconduct.'

GRACE. They can't do that...

BEVERLEY. Say no pay... because I was on probation...

CHERYL. Jesus wept...

GRACE. Fucking bastards?!

BEVERLEY. I dunno what I'm gonna do...

CHERYL. It's alright, love...

GRACE. You've done nothing wrong –

BEVERLEY. But they're saying I have –

GRACE. You've done nothing, except stand up for what you believe in... for your girls...

BEVERLEY. I know –

GRACE. You're not gonna be bullied like this, are ya, Bev?

CHERYL. I won't let them –

GRACE. It's despicable –

BEVERLEY. But... I don't know... if I... what's gonna happen if I come, maybe, maybe I shouldn't –

GRACE. What's gonna happen if you don't? They're saying you don't deserve a voice but you do...

BEVERLEY. But –

CHERYL. I'm gonna keep you safe, I promise you that, girl...

BEVERLEY. Are you sure?

CHERYL. Acourse I am, and Grace...

GRACE. Yeah...

BEVERLEY. Thank you...

CHERYL. Now come on, Wend's running late, we got to do more banners. (*To* GRACE.) Why don't you load the cab up with these bits, eh? And it might need de-icing again... I got a de-icer in me bag if you want it?

GRACE. Yeah. Cheers. I'll be back in a minute... how much longer you reckon on these?

CHERYL. Not long...

GRACE. Alright...

GRACE *exits*.

CHERYL *and* BEVERLEY *paint banners*.

Silence.

CHERYL. You alright now?

BEVERLEY. Yeah... yeah...

CHERYL. I'm dead proud of you...

BEVERLEY *smiles*.

BEVERLEY. Looks proper good that you know... 'fucking'.

CHERYL. Ah cheers, Bev...

BEVERLEY. I really like doing this as it happens. I really like doing it with you... even more than bingo...

CHERYL *puts her arm around* BEVERLEY *and squeezes her*.

CHERYL. I can't get over Wendy, she should be here by now... not like her is it – ?

BEVERLEY. No...

CHERYL. I think this might be it, people might actually listen...

BEVERLEY. I hope so...

CHERYL. I had a woman chase me round Lidl, the other day... so you're not the only one...

BEVERLEY. Oh God –

CHERYL. 'Bigot!' 'Far-right cunt!'

BEVERLEY. Jesus Christ...

CHERYL. Danny were with me an' all –

BEVERLEY. Did he give her what for?

CHERYL *laughs*.

CHERYL. He bloody walked away... down the lucky-dip aisle, buried his head in the Sudoku books and the long johns...

BEVERLEY. Oh no…

CHERYL. I were more annoyed with him than the woman. I told
her: 'Get your ugly ignorant cakehole out of my way,' and she
did – !

BEVERLEY. Oh gosh…

CHERYL. Anyone comes to you, Bev, you tell them to come
straight to me.

BEVERLEY. Okay…

CHERYL. Danny… (*Snorts.*) All Danny keeps saying is:
'You're not to go no more, you're being selfish and I forbid
ya!' Right nasty, in me face –

BEVERLEY. You alright?

CHERYL. Yeah… course I was… told him to fuck off an' all…
at least I'm doing something… He don't even know I'm here
today… ain't spoken to him for days… he's had to find that
cutlery drawer now I tell ya… and his pants are all crusty…

BEVERLEY. Oh, that's not nice…

CHERYL. Ain't even got the sense to turn them inside out… let
alone operate the washing machine…

Beat.

I tried telling him about Grace 'n' all … about how clever
and how brave she is… you know don't ya, how we can
follow her…

WENDY *enters.*

WENDY. Sorry I'm late… the kids –

CHERYL. We've had to do emergency banners because of you…

WENDY. I've got them –

CHERYL. Oh right, well, give them here, because Grace
will want them, she's done such a good job organising
everything –

WENDY. Yeah –

CHERYL. I was just saying to Bev, she's got us all going and you know hope... proper hope... I think she's wonderful. Really, I do...

WENDY. Look, Cheryl, you ain't known Grace that long and –

BEVERLEY. And Grace isn't as good at the dinners as you... Doesn't put enough salt in –

WENDY. It'll be Cheryl, day after next...

CHERYL. Sausage roll and chips...

BEVERLEY. Lovely, ta.

Beat.

I ain't got nothing to be ashamed of, have I...?

WENDY. What you talking about...?

BEVERLEY. The food, the clothes –

WENDY. Get away with ya –

BEVERLEY. I mean it –

CHERYL (*to* BEVERLEY). We're helping out our mate...

BEVERLEY. I'm suspended from work, Wend –

WENDY. You what?!

BEVERLEY. For going up the council with you lot –

CHERYL (*to* BEVERLEY). I told you I'm sorting it –

WENDY. Hang on –

BEVERLEY. And I done something else silly...

CHERYL. What?!

BEVERLEY. I can't get on top of my loan –

CHERYL. But we sat down and we went through it all...

BEVERLEY. I know, but I saw another one on the iPad, better interest rate...

WENDY. Oh, Bev...

CHERYL. Are you stupid?!

BEVERLEY. Don't be cross at me...

CHERYL. I ain't cross. I'm bloody furious...

WENDY (*to* CHERYL). Eh! Don't be like that to her –

GRACE *enters*.

GRACE. Right! (*To* WENDY.) Oh... thought you weren't
coming –

WENDY. Oh, I'm coming alright...

GRACE. That's good, that's good then...

CHERYL. You all set?

GRACE. Yeah...

CHERYL. Got your burqa?

GRACE. Yeah –

CHERYL. Wanna practise your speech?

GRACE. I'll do it in the cab –

CHERYL. Got our T-shirt underneath –

GRACE. Yep –

WENDY (*to* BEVERLEY). We'll talk on the way up –

BEVERLEY *nods her head*.

GRACE *lifts up her jacket and shows a T-shirt which reads:*
'Anti-Extremism Mutineer Women.'

You changed it?

GRACE. What?

WENDY. Mutineer –

CHERYL. I changed it, Grace asked me to get new ones
printed –

GRACE. Cos that's what we are... innit, girls? COME ON!
MUTINEERS!

GRACE/CHERYL. MUTINEERS! MUTINEERS!
MUTINEERS!

Scene Six

CHERYL *stands alone and drinks Archers*. BEVERLEY, GRACE *and* WENDY *enter*.

BEVERLEY. Oh thank God, thanks to God, to Jesus to Mary and the bloody Donkey and all...

WENDY. Where've you been?!

BEVERLEY. You alright?!

CHERYL. I got arrested!

BEVERLEY. Oh, Cherl –

CHERYL. What?!

BEVERLEY. Are you alright?!

CHERYL. I'm fine... I'm absolutely fine, Bev... collateral damage... for the cause, for the unit...

GRACE. Thank you –

WENDY. Some fucking unit...

GRACE. What?

GRACE *turns to directly face* WENDY.

Say it louder... so everyone can hear...

WENDY. You went rogue... you lost it out there!

GRACE. I didn't lose nothing –

WENDY. It was all pointless... don't mean nothing... nobody got the message...

GRACE. They wouldn't let me finish –

WENDY. You had them, you fucking had them –

GRACE. When I had the burqa on?! Exactly, ain't that fucking rich eh? They weren't fucking listening to me when I took it off, to the next part, to our part –

WENDY. So somehow you come to the conclusion that you should burn it, burn the burqa right in the middle of Antifa!?

CHERYL. Got their attention, didn't it – ?!

WENDY. What's the matter with you eh, Cheryl?! Got her a fat lip, could have got us all killed –

GRACE. Bit of blood, so what, so fucking what –

WENDY. Fucking idiot, fucking wreck –

CHERYL. They wouldn't let her speak?!

GRACE. And you didn't hear, what they was chanting right in me ear...

WENDY. Yes I did, we all did... 'Racist, bigot' ain't nothing we ain't used to –

GRACE. In my ear. 'Traitor to your race.'

Beat.

Did you hear that?!

WENDY. Nah, I didn't...

GRACE. I didn't think so... I was defending myself. I was defending us... you saw... you saw... they came at us first... Got it on your phone?

WENDY. No. I didn't.

GRACE. What?! What the fuck?! You had one job, fucking film it –

WENDY. I didn't want to film it, alright? Because it didn't look good, none of it looked any good. (*To* BEVERLEY *and* CHERYL.) Did it? Did it, Bev?

BEVERLEY *shakes her head.*

CHERYL *stares at* WENDY *and shrugs.*

We ain't violent –

GRACE. I didn't start it –

WENDY. First rule –

GRACE. So what... you were just gonna stand there and take it... What happens when they throw the first punch?!

WENDY. I don't know if they did –

GRACE. They fucking did –

GRACE *reels*.

You give it all the biggun, but you ain't got the actions. You're a coward, Wend –

CHERYL (*indicating her phone*). It's all over the news… 'Clashes at UK Hate Hate.' 'Newly formed EDL splinter-group members.' 'Anti-Extremism Mutineer Women.' 'Twelve arrests.'

GRACE. Eleven of them ain't even us; eleven of them are fucking Antifa!

WENDY. Well, it don't say that because it never does! Exactly the opposite of what we stand for… you've gone and done it… gone and provided it to them –

GRACE. But it's a lie!

WENDY. Don't matter, it's out there now!

GRACE. You didn't have to come, Wend –

WENDY. It's my group!

GRACE. You were nothing before me, far-right fucking Calendar Girls…

BEVERLEY. No one got naked – ?!

WENDY (*to* GRACE). We're not far-right. We're not. Never were and now what… we're aligned with the EDL, how the fuck are we EVER gonna be taken seriously now?! You seen my Twitter?!

GRACE. No –

WENDY. Well, let me show ya –

WENDY *pulls out her phone*.

Oh yeah… here we go… 'Nazi', 'Racist', 'Nazi', 'Lock up this white chav, Nazi, racist cunt'.

Beat.

(*To herself*.) Burning the burqa…

WENDY *scoffs*.

Our message is about radical Islam, that's the one thing we fucking had... say goodbye to that... say goodbye to this place... of any chance we had of saving it – !

GRACE. Yeah well...

WENDY. 'Yeah well'?! Yeah fucking well?!

GRACE. If you can't say anything, if being hateful is the only way you're gonna be heard then that's what you've got to become –

WENDY. It's not how *I* operate. I know that fighting don't work –

GRACE. But maybe that's what it'll need to come down to, in the end –

WENDY. I'm suspending the meetings from now on –

GRACE. If you can't hack it, I'll take control –

WENDY. Bev... let's me and Cheryl get you home, eh?

BEVERLEY *picks up her bag*.

GRACE. You quitting then, Bev?

BEVERLEY. I'm sorry...

WENDY. Ain't got nothing to be sorry for...

BEVERLEY. Me girls...

GRACE. Thought that's what you were doing it for... 'Me girls'...

BEVERLEY. I'll see ya, yeah... I'll see ya... come on, Cherl...

Beat.

Shall we go, Cheryl...?

CHERYL. Nah you're alright...

WENDY. You're not gonna stay and listen to her, are ya?

CHERYL (*to* GRACE). It felt good watching you kick the shit outta that bloke... he bloody deserved it...

BEVERLEY. Cheryl…

CHERYL. I didn't jump in to try and save ya… I jumped in to join ya…

BEVERLEY. Cheryl… Please…

CHERYL. You go… get home to your girls… I'm gonna stay here for a bit…

WENDY. Meetings are suspended, there won't be one next week…

CHERYL. Yeah, I heard ya, but the thing is, this one ain't done yet…

WENDY. What's happened to you, eh…?

WENDY *and* BEVERLEY *go to exit.*

GRACE. You take care, Wend, yeah –

WENDY. What's that supposed to mean?

GRACE. I'm just reminding ya, your face, wearing the same T-shirt as me… it's on the article too… ain't small fry now…

Silence.

WENDY *grabs* BEVERLEY*'s hand.*

WENDY. S'alright… s'alright…

WENDY *and* BEVERLEY *exit.*

GRACE. Any of that Archers left, Cherl?

From a plastic bag, CHERYL *pulls another bottle of Archers Peach Schnapps.*

Eh!

CHERYL *hands the bottle to* GRACE, GRACE *swigs and hands the bottle to* CHERYL, CHERYL *swigs.*

Maybe we should turn the music up right loud… and get shitfaced, eh…

CHERYL. Ain't nowhere near enough for how much I want to get shitfaced…

GRACE *goes to the CD player, plays some music, 'Agadoo'
by Black Lace.*

Oh my God! Is anyone ever gonna change that bloody Black
Lace CD?!

GRACE *dances a little.*

GRACE. I don't mind it, me...

CHERYL. Your face, it's bruised...

CHERYL *takes the bottle from GRACE and turns the music
down a little.*

CHERYL *retrieves a first-aid kit from the kitchen, she goes
to GRACE.*

Let me sort you out...

CHERYL *gently attends to GRACE's wounds.*

GRACE *lovingly holds CHERYL's hand as CHERYL
continues to clean the wounds.*

Silence.

There you go... all better...

GRACE *begins to dance.*

CHERYL *joins her.*

GRACE *and CHERYL dance together for a moment.*

After a while, SHELLEY *rushes in, breathless.*

SHELLEY (*to GRACE*). State of you...

GRACE. What you doing here?

SHELLEY. Are you alright...?

GRACE. I'm fine...

SHELLEY. I seen the videos –

GRACE. Cheryl's fixed me up, ain't ya...

CHERYL. Hello...

GRACE. This is erm, well this... is Cheryl... this is... this is
me sister...

CHERYL. Oh, hello.

GRACE. Shelley –

CHERYL. Hi –

SHELLEY. Hi.

CHERYL. Nice to meet you –

SHELLEY. Yeah. This is fucking weird.

GRACE (*to* CHERYL). Sorry, sorry about her...

GRACE *laughs*.

Cheryl's my mate... we been out there... together... on the front line haven't we, eh?

CHERYL. Got a bit vicious –

GRACE. Nothing I couldn't handle...

SHELLEY. What the hell were you doing?

GRACE. You wanna drink?

SHELLEY. Grace –

GRACE. What she's done for me my sis... she's done amazing for me...

CHERYL. Oh, that's nice...

GRACE. I mean it, proper... amazing...

SHELLEY. Why don't you come with me, eh?

GRACE. Cheryl...

CHERYL. Yes, love...

GRACE. I haven't told you something...

CHERYL. Oh, right...

GRACE. Yeah...

CHERYL. What's that then...?

GRACE (*to* SHELLEY). Have you got a picture?

SHELLEY. Erm –

GRACE. Show us –

SHELLEY. Grace –

GRACE. Go on…

SHELLEY. Will ya –

GRACE. Come on –

> GRACE *snatches* SHELLEY's *mobile phone from* SHELLEY's *hand.*

SHELLEY. I think you should come with me –

> GRACE *snatches the phone.*

GRACE. Ta –

> GRACE *looks at the picture, thrusts the phone at* CHERYL.

That's my, that's my girl…

CHERYL. Oh…?

GRACE. Yeah…

CHERYL. Oh, Grace…

GRACE. That's my Esme, that is…

CHERYL. Oh, you never said…

GRACE. No, well, erm, well, Shelley's been doing the looking after –

CHERYL. She's absolutely beautiful… knockout…

> CHERYL *hands the phone back to* GRACE, GRACE *smiles, stares at the photo.*

GRACE. 'Very light-skinned, too beautiful to be yours.'

CHERYL. Eh?

GRACE. What some woman said to me at hospital… tricked me… 'What a lovely, lovely baby.' Then turned looked at me… suspicious… 'Is it yours?!' –

CHERYL. That's not very nice –

GRACE. No, no it ain't, is it…

SHELLEY. I told you that was bollocks. You know she's yours –

GRACE. Do you know what, today, I've been thinking… I've been doing a lot of thinking and as of right now… I would like to come and see her…

SHELLEY. Erm…?

GRACE. You know, like you said, like you said before –

SHELLEY. Right…

GRACE. I could come right now with you, eh… just for a little while… and Cheryl… Cheryl too… if you like?

CHERYL. Can do… that'd be nice…

GRACE. She's lovely, our Cherl… she knits, doncha? Does she need a hat?

SHELLEY. Erm –

CHERYL. I got a tape measure in my bag, could come and measure her little head…

SHELLEY. The thing is… I think your face… it might scare her…

GRACE. Oh –

SHELLEY. Yeah –

GRACE. Another time, soon –

SHELLEY. Maybe –

GRACE. What'd you mean 'maybe'?

Beat.

She's my daughter… I want to tell her all what I'm doing for her…

SHELLEY. And erm… what is that… exactly?

CHERYL *raises her glass in the air and drinks.*

CHERYL. Mutineering – !

GRACE. Yeah! Mutineering!

SHELLEY. Mutineering...? Mutineering for what...?

GRACE. Making her safe... from radical Islam... from Islam...

SHELLEY. There's nothing wrong with Islam!

GRACE. Yes there is – !

SHELLEY. No there isn't – !

GRACE. Today's the first day I haven't seen it... the fear,
today's the day it's gone... from in here... I am in control
now... because I've realised in Afghan... I just wanted to,
in his last minute... his last moment... squeeze... squeeze
a bit... squeeze a little bit of love in... a little boy... I didn't
kill him... he wouldn't have lived... the bomb killed him...
I ran in and I squeezed the love into him... cos he were
smiling just before and somehow... somehow... he kept that
smile... and I've thought all this time, that after I squeezed
him, I squeezed the smile out of him... killed him... but I
didn't... did I? I was squeezing the love in...

CHERYL. Oh my God...

SHELLEY. Grace...

GRACE. So there you go... It weren't me... it were them what
done it... and I am gonna stop that from ever happening
here –

SHELLEY. Let me help you...

GRACE. I wanna see her...

SHELLEY. Grace –

GRACE. I'm okay now –

SHELLEY. But you're not... you're really not... You got it all
messed up in here... you can't just hate... a whole religion...
a community... You're not a racist, Grace?

GRACE. You don't get it –

SHELLEY. But it fucking well looks like you are… what you've done… what you're saying is racist and I don't understand…

GRACE. Then join us; we need more women like you, women that wanna fight, make a stand. Do it for Esme –

SHELLEY. I used to be so proud of you, my big sister… I love you… but I don't know who you are no more… I'm ashamed of you –

GRACE. Piss off –

SHELLEY. Why would you wanna do that?! Don't you think Muslims get enough shit, go through enough suffering?!

GRACE. Give me my girl –

SHELLEY. Your dad was Muslim, Grace…

GRACE. What the fuck did you just say?! You've absolutely no fucking idea about me… I am not that –

SHELLEY. Nana might have thought she was protecting you, telling you to fear Muslim men, brown men, that one might be your dad, and he might steal you away from her… but she was wrong and she was grieving for Mum…

GRACE. I want my girl back!

SHELLEY. You think anyone in their right mind will let you near… when they see you on that video…?!

GRACE *grabs* SHELLEY *by the scruff of the neck.*

GRACE. Don't… don't make me something for her to be terrified of an' all…

GRACE *lets go of* SHELLEY.

Beat.

SHELLEY *breaks down.*

SHELLEY. I'm sorry… I'm so sorry, but until you sort yourself out, Grace, I can't let you see her…

Beat.

GRACE. Shelley!

>SHELLEY *exits*.

>GRACE *collapses into* CHERYL*'s arms*.

CHERYL. Come here... come here... love...

GRACE (*whispering*). She's mine...

CHERYL. I know...

GRACE. I just want my girl...

CHERYL. It's okay –

GRACE. What's the point in all this, eh? If she won't let me near –

CHERYL. Don't be fucking silly now.

>GRACE *reels*.

GRACE. I dunno...

CHERYL (*in close to* GRACE). Everything you're fighting for is for your girl... and she'll thank you one day for keeping her safe...

>*Beat*.

We're not going down like this, are we?!

>*Beat*.

GRACE. No... no...

Scene Seven

The CD player plays a crackled, broken version of 'The Birdie Song' by Black Lace.

GRACE *is setting up banner material and paint. An expensive-looking suitcase sits near her.*

A knock at the door.

GRACE *goes to the door and listens.*

CHERYL (*through the door*). It's me, Cheryl...

> GRACE *unlocks the door.*

> CHERYL *enters carrying a large bag,* BEVERLEY *follows her.*

> GRACE *locks the door.*

> Alright?

GRACE. Yeah, you?

CHERYL. Yeah. I got long-life milk, energy bars and shitloads of nuts, keep our strength up –

GRACE. Cheers.

> GRACE *takes the bags from* CHERYL, *including her handbag and chucks it in the cupboard.*

> You alright, Bev?

BEVERLEY. Hello...

GRACE. You want a cuppa?

BEVERLEY. Is that your nice suitcase, Cheryl?

CHERYL. Yeah...

BEVERLEY. What you got that for...?

CHERYL. Well, Danny don't need it and I don't need Danny –

GRACE. I'm so glad you came, Bev –

BEVERLEY. She said I had to –

GRACE. Cos we need you... now –

BEVERLEY. Lost me job... Won't even let me in the school grounds to pick the girls up... I had to meet them round the corner; they crossed that busy road on their own...

GRACE. What?!

BEVERLEY. I feel like a kiddie-fiddler or something...

CHERYL. The way they've treated her –

GRACE. It's despicable. I'm sorry, Bev...

BEVERLEY. I...

GRACE. We gotta keep fighting, we can't give up now. Let's get you on banners with Cherl, I've set it all up –

CHERYL. Righto –

BEVERLEY. What... what are we doing?

GRACE. A lock-in... we're gonna fly banners outside to protest the demolition. Can't knock this place down with us in it. I want everyone of you on a door... no one is getting in –

WENDY *enters, using her keys.*

You came... come in, sit yourself down –

WENDY. Come on, Bev, I've got dinner on for us at home.

Beat.

Bev, these two have just got in your head.

BEVERLEY. Nobody's got in me head... I need some help is all...

CHERYL (*to* BEVERLEY). You're alright –

WENDY (*to* BEVERLEY). Come with me, love...

GRACE. That's not being a team player, is it?!

WENDY (*to* BEVERLEY *and* CHERYL). You're coming, aren't ya?

GRACE. I'm trying to fucking well protect you, Wend... protect you all... But fuck it, give me your keys and get out!

WENDY. You don't have to do this... Let's stop it... eh?

GRACE. You giving up, just like that?!

WENDY. What are you dragging them into now – ?!

CHERYL. She ain't dragging us into nothing –

GRACE. Are you scared of being called a racist, Wend? You're scared just like the rest of the white liberals, eh?

GRACE *laughs*.

Perhaps we should talk about the big brown elephant in the room – ?!

Beat.

You more or less handpicked me. Your fucking poster girl...

WENDY. We could have made people actually hear us –

GRACE. Legitimacy that you're not racist. I can be brown on the outside and white on the inside... so just fucking say it... once and for all, say how much you hate them all... say it, say it, SAY IT!

WENDY *grabs* GRACE.

CHERYL *tries to intercept*.

CHERYL. What THE FUCK do you think you're doing?!

WENDY *lets* GRACE *go*.

WENDY *breaks down*.

WENDY (*to* GRACE). I'm sorry... (*To the room.*) I'm so sorry...

GRACE. You are a racist... cos picking me... bringing me in... that was the most racist thing you've ever done...

Beat.

I've really got to get stuff ready with the troops –

CHERYL. What is it you bang on about all the time? 'Peace', well, there ain't no peace... I choose hate.

BEVERLEY. Cheryl... enough's... enough?

CHERYL. Sit down then –

BEVERLEY. Cherl –

CHERYL. Sit –

BEVERLEY. I…

CHERYL. Ah your girls…

WENDY. Be braver than this –

CHERYL. Fuck you. I am being brave.

BEVERLEY. Cherl…?!

CHERYL. I got a nice sausage casserole that I were bringing over later…

BEVERLEY. What you saying…?

CHERYL. Did you like the bangers and mash? Did you like the chilli hot dogs? Did you like the toad-in-the-hole? Wendy she's always that busy, with her own girls…

Beat.

I'm just asking… if you liked it?!

BEVERLEY. I…

BEVERLEY *tears up.*

BEVERLEY *sits.*

WENDY. Bev… get up… Get up!

BEVERLEY *shakes her head.*

WENDY *breaks down.*

Fucking hell…

WENDY *exits, dropping her keys on the floor as she does so.*

GRACE *locks the door behind her.*

GRACE. Right… we all set then?! Yeah… we're all set…

CHERYL *returns to painting banners.*

GRACE *goes to a bag and pulls out some petrol cans and rags.*

Right, how much longer on the banners?

CHERYL. Not long…

GRACE. Well, I need someone on this with me… Bev, can you come over here…

BEVERLEY goes to GRACE.

GRACE hands BEVERLEY some rags.

Get dunking those please…

BEVERLEY slowly starts to dunk the rags.

BEVERLEY. What… what are these for, Grace…?

GRACE. For setting this place alight…

BEVERLEY. We ain't doing that, are we…?

GRACE. Yeah, yeah we are –

BEVERLEY. Why…?!

GRACE. Sending a statement…

BEVERLEY. Statement…?

GRACE. Yes… we don't want it to go to them –

BEVERLEY. This erm, this petrol, it's getting into my head… Cheryl…?

GRACE. Come on, Cheryl…

CHERYL walks over to BEVERLEY and GRACE.

GRACE hands rags to CHERYL.

A statement and a means to an end. Can't develop it if it's incinerated.

BEVERLEY. But what if we hurt someone…

GRACE. There are always casualties in war, Bev…

BEVERLEY. I can't… I can't hurt no one…

Beat.

Cheryl, you can't do that?!

Silence.

I'm sorry… but I… no…

CHERYL. Bev –

BEVERLEY. No, no way – !

GRACE. Alright fine, piss off then, give us your rags!

GRACE *snatches* BEVERLEY*'s rags, knocking cakes and petrol everywhere.*

BEVERLEY. I'm not leaving without you, Cheryl, not this time…

CHERYL. I have to, for my Liz –

BEVERLEY (*pointing to* GRACE). She's not bloody her!

Beat.

I'm sorry…

Beat.

Even if she were… she wouldn't want you killing…

GRACE. Don't listen to her, Cherl, don't let her get in your head –

CHERYL. Shut up!

CHERYL *breaks down.*

She ain't coming is she… she ain't coming through that door…

BEVERLEY. No…

BEVERLEY *tries to comfort* CHERYL, *but* CHERYL *pushes her away.*

CHERYL. I've been waiting for her all this time… but she ain't coming…

BEVERLEY *persists, she gently rocks* CHERYL.

Silence.

BEVERLEY. Come on, love… let's get out of here, eh…

CHERYL *and* BEVERLEY *stand.*

GRACE. Don't go.

Beat.

Please don't go.

CHERYL. I'm sorry…

GRACE. Don't fucking leave me!

Beat.

We're fighting! We're fighting together!

Beat.

They want us to sit down and shut up!

CHERYL *puts her hand out to* GRACE.

GRACE *bats it away.*

Traitors! Fucking! COWARDS!

CHERYL *exits briefly to the cupboard and grabs her handbag.*

BEVERLEY *and* GRACE *briefly stand alone.*

Bev…

A knock at the door.

BEVERLEY *rushes to the door and opens it.*

SHELLEY *barges in.*

SHELLEY. Where is she?! GRACE! Where is Esme?!

GRACE. What you talking about!?

SHELLEY. WHERE THE FUCK IS SHE?!

GRACE. You gone and lost her?!

SHELLEY. Jesus fucking Christ… What the hell have you done with her?! Grace! Please! Please… (*To* BEVERLEY.) Is she here…? Has she got the baby here…?!

BEVERLEY. Baby…? What baby?

GRACE. Lost my baby girl?!

SHELLEY. Please, please just hand her over, Grace! I won't go
police... please just let me have her...

GRACE. What kind of mother are you, eh? To lose a baby – ?!

SHELLEY. I... no, no... I didn't... I...?! She was in the cot...
we were asleep right next to each other...

CHERYL returns holding a baby.

CHERYL. She was in the cupboard, Grace...

SHELLEY runs to Esme and takes her from CHERYL.

SHELLEY. Give her here!

SHELLEY cradles Esme in her arms.

S'alright... s'alright...

Beat.

GRACE. We have to protect our own...

SHELLEY. Look at her...

GRACE shakes her head.

SHELLEY holds Esme up to GRACE. GRACE pulls away.

GRACE. I've got to protect her...

SHELLEY. She's so scared... she's trying not to cry... because
she's so scared of you, look at her...

GRACE stares at Esme.

GRACE. Is she...?

GRACE turns away.

Oh... oh...

SHELLEY. Let me help you...

GRACE. I...

SHELLEY. Grace, I love you... please, please let me try...

Beat.

GRACE nods.

GRACE. Okay… okay…

Beat.

Shelley, what am I doing…?

SHELLEY. You're Grace… and this; this is your beautiful little girl…

SHELLEY *gently places Esme in* GRACE'*s arms.*

GRACE *gently strokes Esme's head.*

GRACE. My girl… my girl…

Fade to black.

The End.

A Nick Hern Book

Heroine first published in Great Britain in 2017 as a paperback original by Nick Hern Books Limited, The Glasshouse, 49a Goldhawk Road, London W12 8QP, in association with HighTide and Theatr Clwyd

Heroine copyright © 2017 Nessah Muthy

Nessah Muthy has asserted her moral right to be identified as the author of this work

Cover photograph by Helen Maybanks. Design by Rebecca Pitt.

Designed and typeset by Nick Hern Books, London
Printed in the UK by Mimeo Ltd, Huntingdon, Cambridgeshire PE29 6XX

A CIP catalogue record for this book is available from the British Library

ISBN 978 1 84842 709 9

Woodland
CARBON
www.woodlandcarbon.co.uk
NICK HERN BOOKS
Printed on Carbon Captured paper

www.nickhernbooks.co.uk

 facebook.com/nickhernbooks

 twitter.com/nickhernbooks